A
LAKE SAMBELL
WALK

Picture Poetry
en plein air

FRANK PREM

Publication Details

Title: *A Lake Sambell Walk*
ISBN: 978-1-925963-69-4 (p-bk)
ISBN: 978-1-925963-70-0 (e-bk)

Published by Wild Arancini Press
2021

come let us walk together

Contents

About
A Lake Sambell Walk

A Lake Sambell Walk is a picture-poetry collection that comes from a gentle wander around a picturesque lake lying at the heart of Beechworth, the town in which I grew up and reside in at the time of writing. Lake Sambell is a man-made remnant of the gold mining era and can be readily circumnavigated on foot.

Taking a stroll around the water on a gorgeous day in 2018, digital camera in hand, I was sufficiently engaged by the elements of what I saw – significant and trivial, both – to create a small collection of poems to accompany the images, and serve as a reminder of the walk.

I hope that you, too, might enjoy a walk around Lake Sambell with me, through the medium of this short-form picture-poetry.

FP

A Lake Sambell Walk

sea above

not a lake . . .

no

it is a sea
in the sky
above

white breakers
stretch
in lines
to their shore . . .

wash
over me

convergence west

shallows
to distant shores

a wake
of duck
surges

clouds
swim to converge
west

mirrored rumor

today

rumours
in the reflections

whispers
of
the other side

mirrored
my way

pleasing

the composition
of sunlight
is
pleasing . . .

laid down
in the distance

grey above

grey below

sunlight
laying down
upon the trees
is . . .

pleasing

castle

a castle
above the cliffs

a rhine idea
on a lake sambell
scale

finding

pinus
radiata crowd the bank

but
there is a way
down there

a way
to find water

scribbled harmony

scribbled sky

reed
and weed
and water

discordant
harmony

yours

up
through your tangled
self . . .

the blue sky
waits

reach tall

be straight

it is yours
if only
you take it

reach tall

take everything
that is yours

thin

thin . . .

too thin

too thin to rain

too little
to storm

too much
to hope for

too thin
to care

armoured heart

water
at the heart
of granite

worn
like a suit
of rocky armour

gloved by no one

was it cold
last night . . .

warm today . . .

who
left them

who
wants them

no one
loves them

there is no one
to glove

future north

over the pines
with the clouds

northward
we roll

breeze take us –
held
in a ripple –
to the other side

the future waits
over there

such a forest

wattle forest

there is no way
through

don't leave the path –
we may never
find you

lost
lost . . .

ah
what a fate

in *such*
a forest

ordinary

how green is that

is it
an ireland green

is it
england

no

just
a lakeside hue

a pine-tree palette

in
an ordinary
shade

coloured hats

big brother

small brother

fun guys
in sundry sizes

party boys
in yellow hats

the everlasting

everlasting
is not
eternal

it is just
a daisy
in her paper skin

next year
she will last forever
again

don't know

who
tumbles these stumps –
these disarrayed branches –
together

why

will there be
a bonfire
set
upon the rippled waves

is this a tidal thing
on an inland lake

flotsam and jetsam
assembled
by the wind

I don't know

I just
do not
know

on a stick

cormorant
on a stick
in the lake
above the water

a little *pied* . . .

a little
black . . .

who knows
what kind you are

just
a minor cormorant
resting
upon a slender stick

serenity seat

take a seat

watch the ducks

admire
the dabchick grebes

serenity
is a soft breeze
upon the lake

ours

don't crowd
boys
don't crowd

there is space
yet
out on the water

all we need do
is spread ourselves
wide

it will all
be ours

tomorrow

willow
weeping
why do you stoop
so low

clouds will pass
sun will shine
tomorrow

and
tomorrow

dabbie shining pictures

swim you dabbies
swim

there are paddlers
over *there*

and *here* . . .

a bumbler
with a camera
set to take too many
too shining
pictures

cut lunch light

the darker hues
make a longer lake
or so
it seems

in sunshine
I could believe
I am circumnavigating
but . . .

in *this* light
it is a journey
that should have brought
its own
cut lunch

south reeds

reeds
will sway

whichever way
the wind blows

south today

pointing me
towards
home

no one will

is there
a fish . . .

perhaps
a cray . . .

should I
dismantle the rock wall
to forage
and to fossick

to find out

if I only move
a few
just to see . . .

perhaps
no one will notice

not long ago

hey!

hey!

is that me
over there on the path . . .

no

not now
but
I *was*

not
so very long
ago

a scattering

the dabchicks
of the scattering
are flung

perhaps
by wind

perhaps
by inclination

far and wide

occasionally
deep

cormorant tree (1)

on the cormorant tree
we watch

we align ourselves

we wait

we dry

cormorant tree (2)

yes
on the cormorant tree
we watch

and wait

and
we dry

cormorant tree (3)

still we watch

still
we wait

still we are
too damp
to leave

to go fishing

cormorant tree (4)

ah
here comes
an entertainment

let's all watch him
alight

while
we wait

while
we watch

while we dry

precious

squeeze

from the heart
comes
a drop
of liquid gold

precious
as life

reaching (of the octo-pine)

a tangle of arms

reaching . . .

thank goodness
it is at
a little distance

and away off
the side
of the road

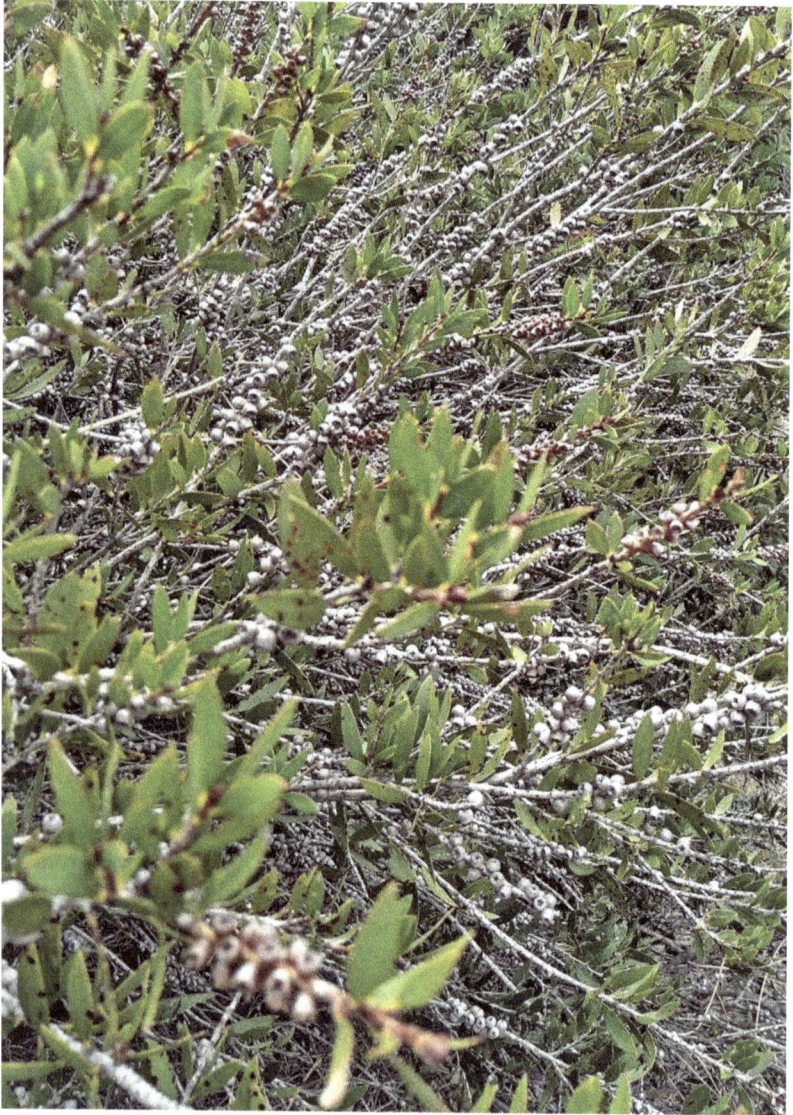

wait a while

seed homes

wait a while
there will be callistemon
flowers

there will be bees

there will be
another season

then
seed homes
and . . .

wait a while

on wet feet

a perspective
leads me down
towards
the water

no
no
no
I
will not go that way

I am not dressed
for a perspective
that might see me
with
my feet wet

when the ovens yellows

you –
I *think* –
are an ovens wattle

dinosaur leaves
and golden flowers
loved
by the *gang gang*
cockatoo

oh
to see you
when you yellow

little smile

little weed . . .

little flower . . .

little
pretty

when I look at you
I see
only
smiling faces

the good, the bad

good
or bad
or
ugly

thistle
what do you think
that *you*
are doing here

too late . . .

old flowers

so wide

hello
big water

big enough to reflect
the shape
that is the sky

you look –
to me –
as wide as a mile

but I recall
once
when I was just
so young

I swam you

only one time

so wide
ago

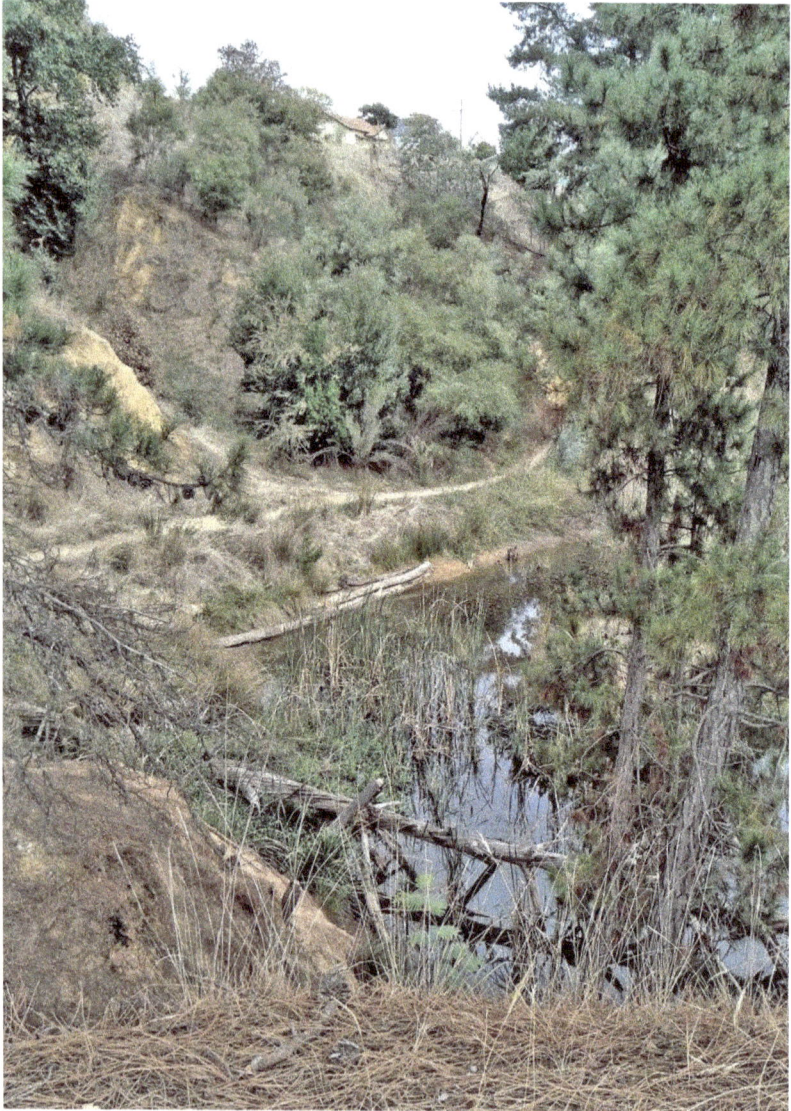

old hole

was there
treasure here
once . . .

there *was* treasure
here

once

they took it all
away
long ago

now
a track
walks the rugged hillside

now
their old hole
is my lake

left when

onward march

below the green

the colour beneath your feet
is the clay
left behind
when the gold
walked away

drawing up ducks

a pipeline
to draw up
ducks
and dabs
from the water

transport them
into
another sphere

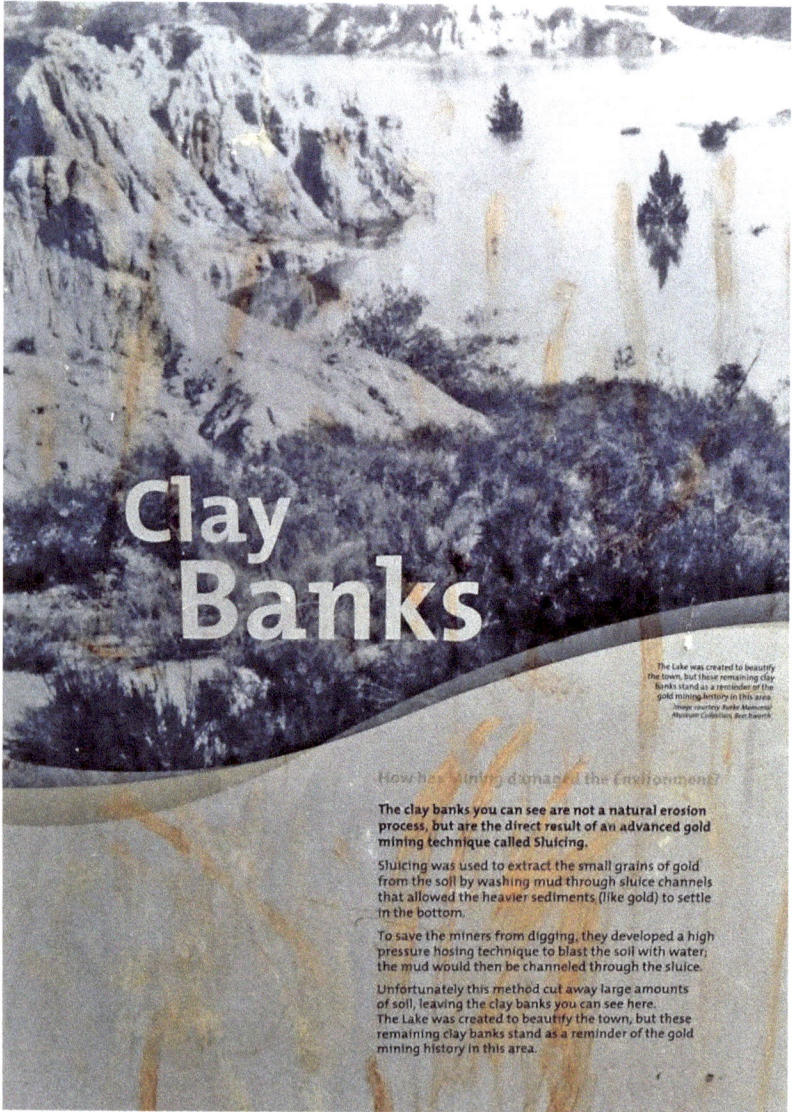

Clay Banks

The Lake was created to beautify the town, but these remaining clay banks stand as a reminder of the gold mining history in this area.
Image courtesy Burke Memorial Museum Collection, Bret Inworth

How has Mining damaged the Environment?

The clay banks you can see are not a natural erosion process, but are the direct result of an advanced gold mining technique called Sluicing.

Sluicing was used to extract the small grains of gold from the soil by washing mud through sluice channels that allowed the heavier sediments (like gold) to settle in the bottom.

To save the miners from digging, they developed a high pressure hosing technique to blast the soil with water; the mud would then be channeled through the sluice.

Unfortunately this method cut away large amounts of soil, leaving the clay banks you can see here. The Lake was created to beautify the town, but these remaining clay banks stand as a reminder of the gold mining history in this area.

still (to this day)

here is the sign that
explains
what happened here

I have seen
the action
in an old movie

big water pushed out
of a giant hose

taking the hills
away

clay fingers
show

there is excavation
going on
right here
to this day

etch moth

the bogong moth
and its *witchety grubs*

who would have thought
I would find one
etched here

into a sign

memory wash

a washaway

the cliff remains
unstable

memories etched anew
each time
it rains

in a hundred

and *there*
is glade beauty

made by the spreading
of oaks

peace
in a place
of old
disruptions

a hundred years more
and no one
will know

taking, not asking

silhouette dabchick

I see you there

I will take
a little
of your soul

for my photograph

thank you
though I was rude
not to ask

leisure (among the dabs)

reeds
and rafts
and panorama

a leisurely day
under the sky

above the water

among
the dabbies

step this way

this way . . .

        step

        step

        step

this way . . .

        step

        step

        step

gold remains (a memory)

almost
the gold
remains

a dignity of form
clinging
through time
that erodes . . .

everything

even –
eventually –
the memory

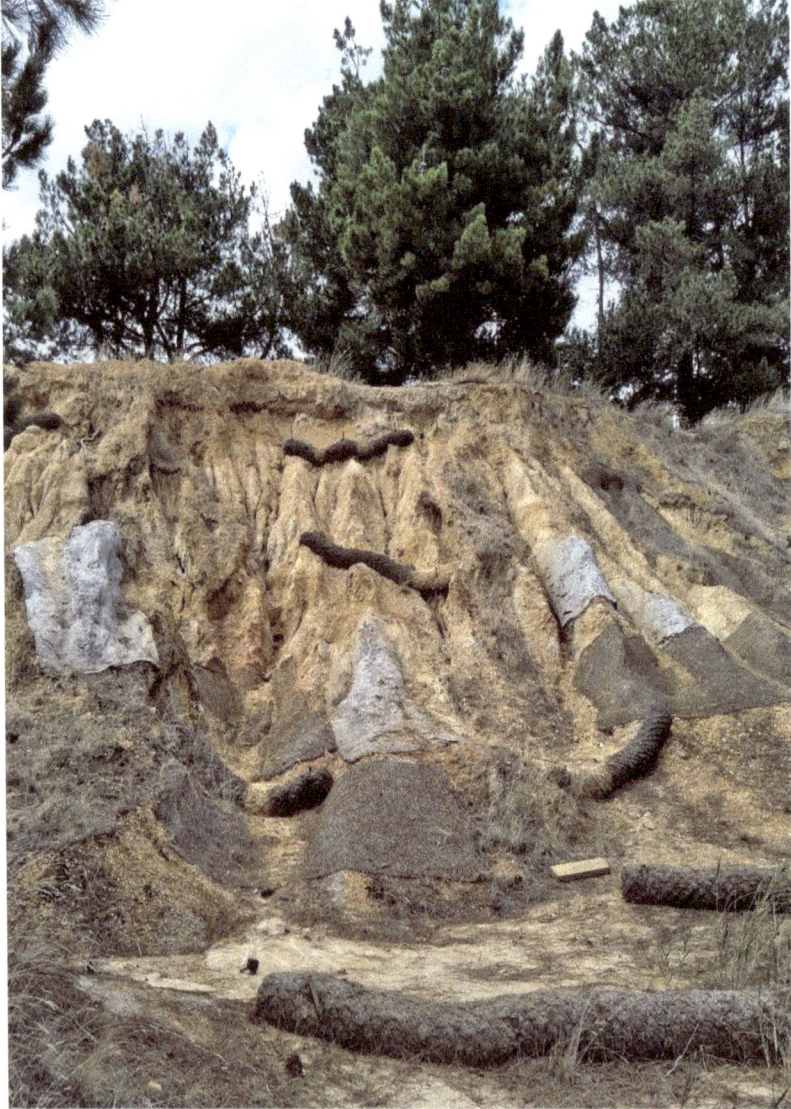

small interest

snakes
and worms
and caterpillars

crawling like
feeders
hungry to consume
the old clay

they
are welcome
for
nothing else
shows
even the smallest
interest

shhhh hiding

peek-a-boo

I look at you
from my hiding place

you don't see me

shhhhh

I . . .

shhhhh

you
don't see me

imagine erosion

rat nest

weed pile

organic material
to block up
a wash-away

just erosion
held back
by a little
imagination

a clear misdirection

ya!

don't tell me
it is not
confusing

lost

I grow lost
in the lines
that run
from here . . .

to there

lost

my eyes
cannot see you

ready

a tuft
at the top
of the bulrush . . .

departs

there is a journey
waiting

ready
to be taken

sausage (on a stick)

anyone care
for a sausage
on a stick?

anyone?

bulrush sausage?

anyone?

attention

that black one
there

standing
to attention

the colour
slides away
against the pink
behind

waiting

I see your heart

I see you
exposed . . .

to *me*

show your
self

I am . . .

I am
waiting

blister

a blister . . .

or . . .

a boil

I know
that you
are there

a pustulation
or a diamond

on my
bark

I know
that there
you are

bow (reunited)

root

where
is your tree

bow down
low

maybe . . .

maybe
it will be revealed

and you
reunited

you
and your tree

an end

is *forever*
something
that a lake knows

or is
forever
just a word to say that
somewhere . . .

somewhere
there will *be*
an end

for my boat

what colour
is this

    candy shop

    chocolate bar

what colour
bonbon
for *my* boat

but the day

how far . . .

so far
from end to end

from *here*
to *there*

it is only water

only sky

with clouds
and birds

from here
to the far end

nothing
at all
but
the day

everything seen

what can you see
in the water

I see
the trees

I see
too
the sky

ripples that roll

I see *everything*

from the water
to me
there is –
reflected –
everything

like autumn

a rummage
of autumn leaves
rolls

across the path

they creep
towards me

just
as autumn
nears

which way

which way
would you go
if the world
allowed

unrestrained
by twists and turns
would you straighten
of your own will

or bend
and flex
around a perceived centre-line
that
only you
can know

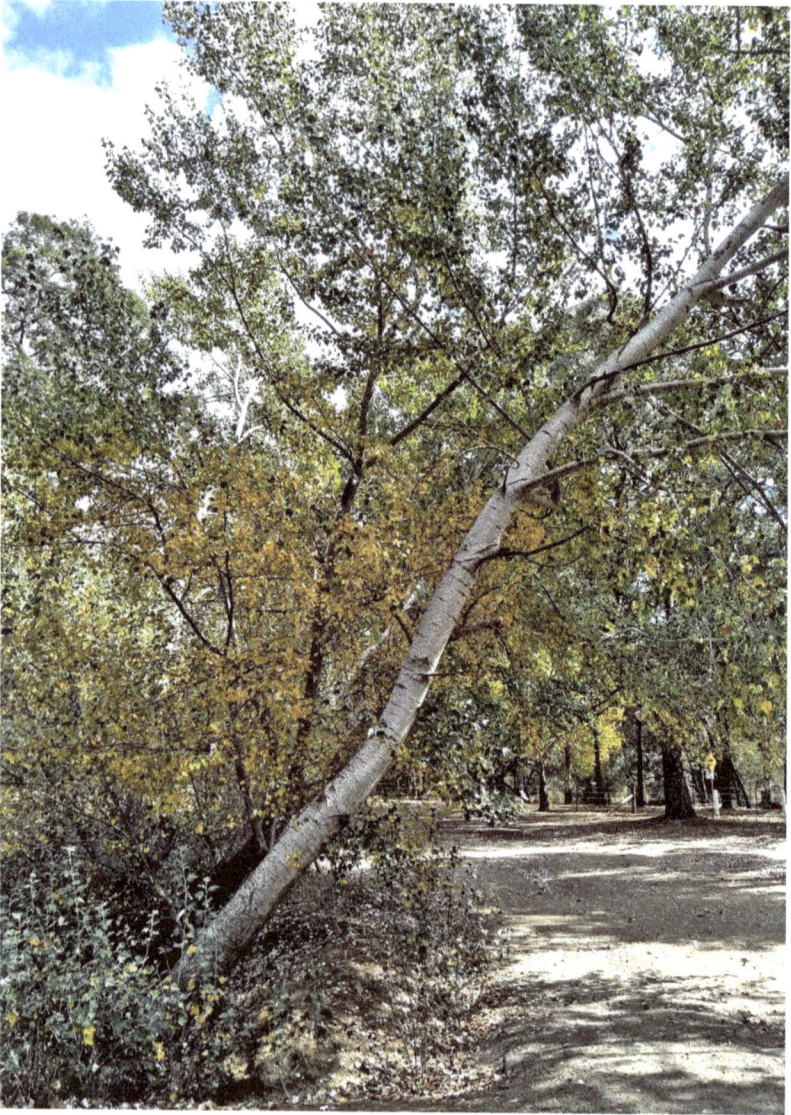

best (to the sky)

it is hard to find
true north
in times of wind

in times
of lean

times
that seem
too troubled

so lay down
your burden

rest
across your shadows

reach
as best you can
for the sky

Thankyou We Hope You Enjoyed Your Stay

LAKE SAMBELL
• CARAVAN PARK •
BEECHWORTH

here (am I)

where am I . . .

here am I

who are *you* . . .

I read you
clearly

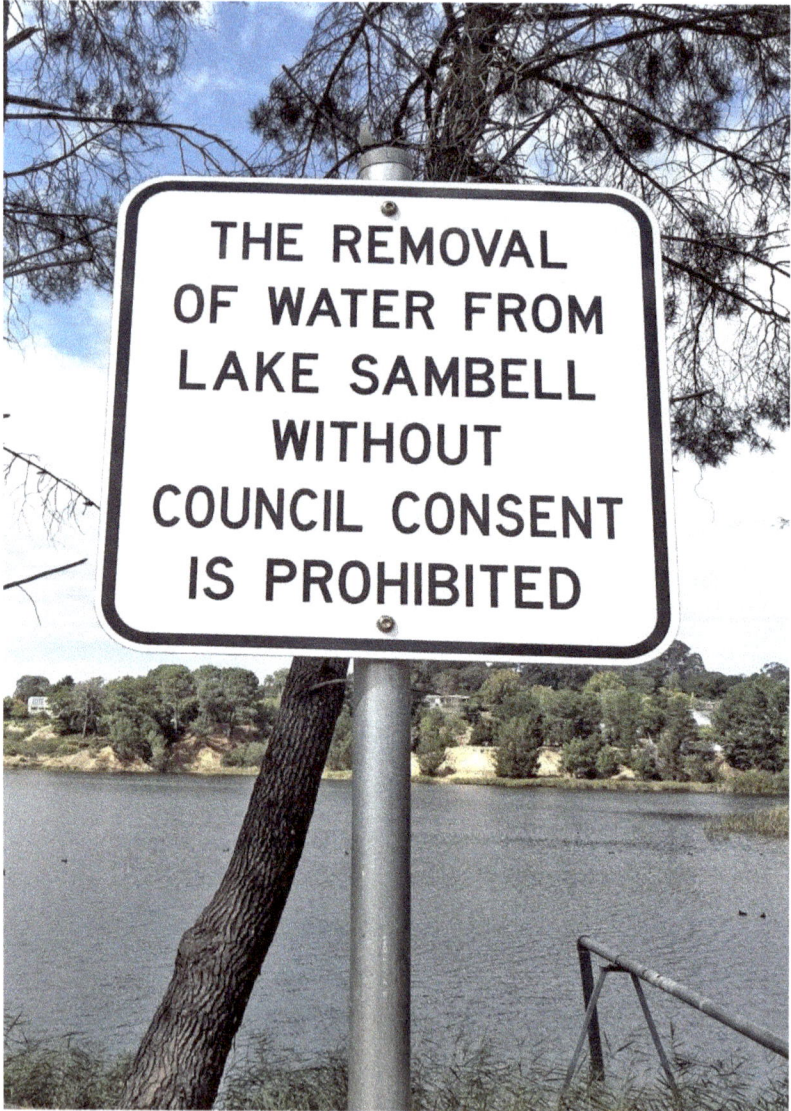

THE REMOVAL
OF WATER FROM
LAKE SAMBELL
WITHOUT
COUNCIL CONSENT
IS PROHIBITED

small theft

and who –
I ask –
would take this
water . . .

some small child
filling up
pockets . . .

no
some large fool
selling it
in plastic bottles

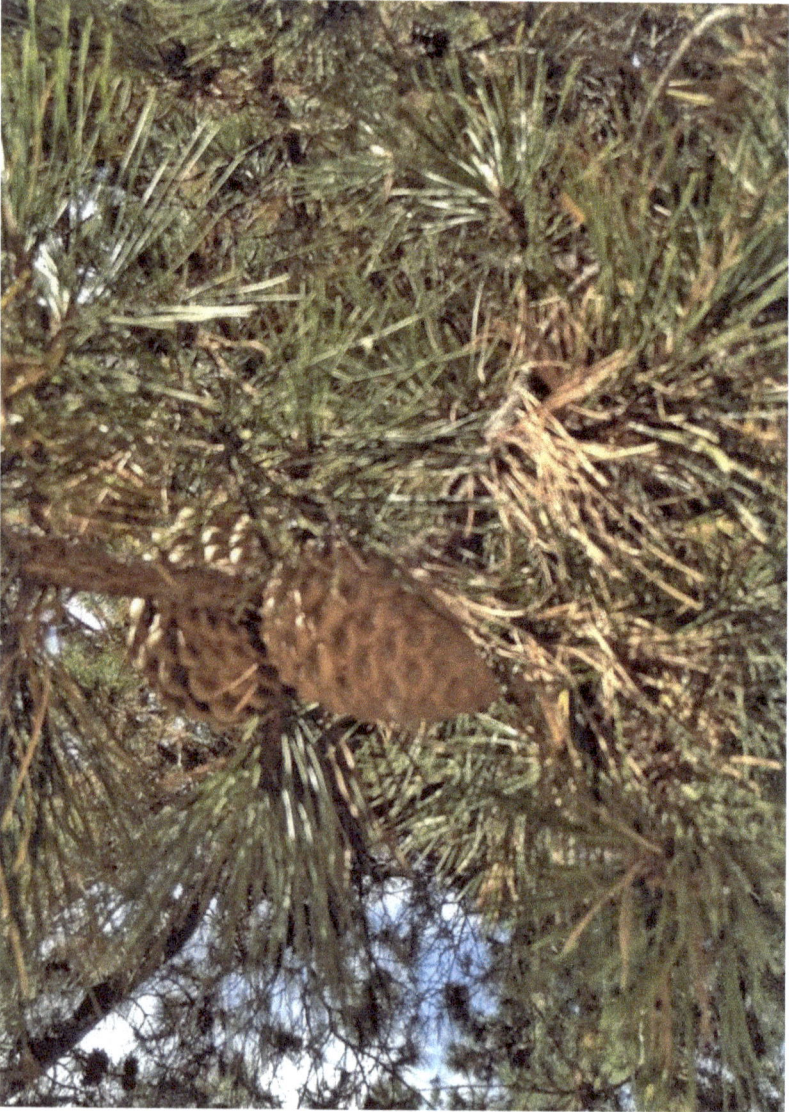

until it is

hold tight
to yourself

winter comes

so
sleep

sleep
until you *feel*
that it is
spring

someone listened

I said
I'd like to have a place
on the lake
where I can park
my bicycle . . .

next thing I know –
just for once –
somebody
listened

like water

down
into the wild
where the granite field
flows

rocks
in a spill
run away
like water

politics of the lake

the road goes on
the rocks
sheer away

there is no
accord

only a marked
divergence

a decoration

the water looks
soft

like a jelly

it ripples
instead of wobbling

holds the reeds
in place
like
a decoration

all

old
and new

the young
the dead
and the dying

from cradle
to grave
this single glimpse
tells me
everything

Trout cod in lakes Kerferd and Sambell

Building new recreational fisheries

In 2006, the Victorian Government began stocking trout cod into lakes Kerferd and Sambell to establish new populations and create a recreational fishery. In 2015, following favourable fish population surveys, the lakes were opened to recreational fishing for the limited harvest of trout cod by anglers.

Creating a trout cod fishery in these lakes, each in public waters and of this species, provide an exciting new recreational fishing experience and introduce a new generation of freshwater anglers to conservation efforts for this species in the wild.

Fishing regulations

For trout cod in lakes Kerferd and Sambell only:
- Minimum size: 40 cm
- Maximum size: 50 cm
- Daily catch & possession limit: 1 fish

The take of trout cod from any other water is an offence under the Fisheries Act 1995 and heavy penalties apply.

158

fish back home

when I
was a lad

the codfish grew
to as long
as four feet

a hundred-pound
fish
was a common
tale

I recall
right here
a skeleton
leaning against a post
at the boat ramp

it frightened me –
that fish –
so badly
I went
home

Distinguishing features of trout cod and Murray cod

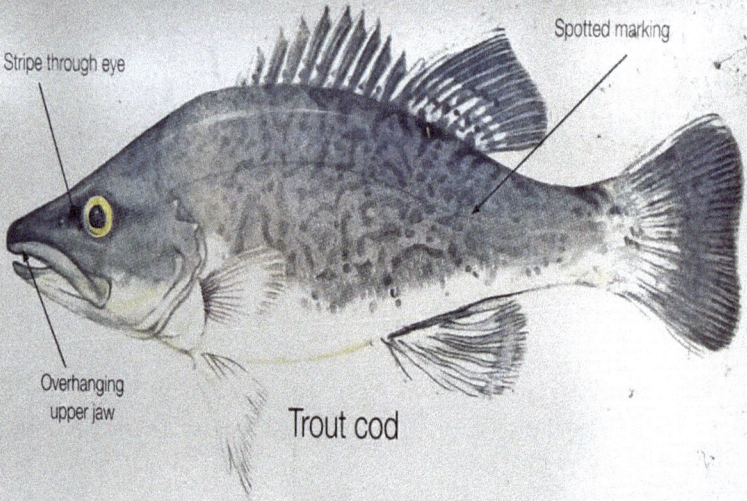

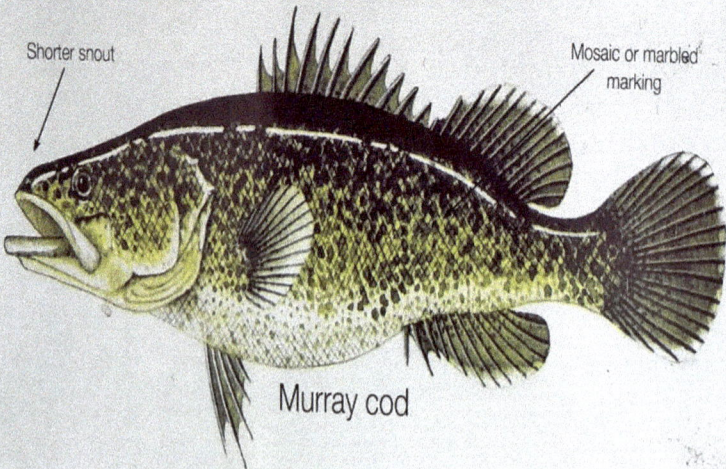

Stripe through eye

Spotted marking

Overhanging upper jaw

Trout cod

Shorter snout

Mosaic or marbled marking

Murray cod

for me

trout cod

whoever heard
of such a thing
as
a *trout cod*

the *old* form
of murray monster
was always good enough
for me

a bardy grub
on a hook . . .

a strong line . . .

a smoke
in my mouth . . .

and some patience

that
was good enough
for me

the occasion

well
well
well
my little dabble-chicks

is there an event . . .

a party . . .

an occasion

nice to see you
gathered
in the one place

it was good of you
all
to come

welcome
my dark dabble-chicks
to this
occasion

little flowers

little flowers

who sees
such
little flowers

down
below my knees
where all the world
is a farther place
live
the little blooms

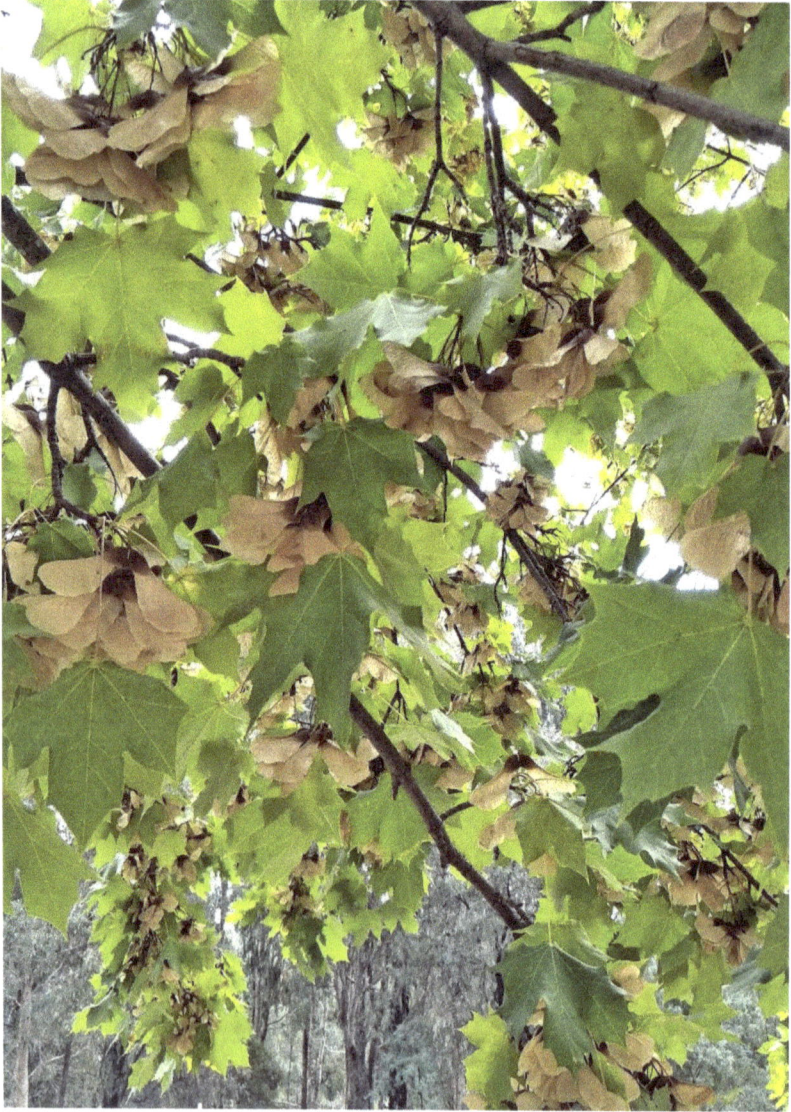

like moths

like moths
they cling
to the underside
of their chosen tree

ready to flutter
away

toward the first
bright
light

dream of flight

friends
are you
sleeping

you are so quiet
I believe you
might be
lost
within a dream

the dream
of flying

Author Information

About the Author

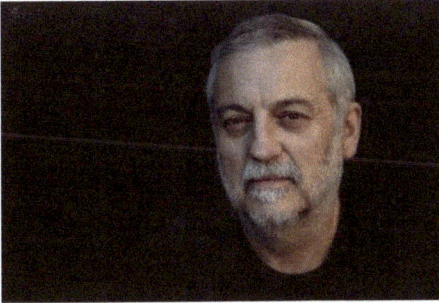

Frank Prem has been a storytelling poet since his teenage years. He has been a psychiatric nurse through all of his professional career, which now exceeds forty years.

He has been published in magazines, online zines, and anthologies in Australia, and in a number of other countries, and has both performed and recorded his work as spoken word.

He lives with his wife in the beautiful township of Beechworth in North-East Victoria, Australia.

Connect with Frank

As the author, I hope you enjoyed this volume of poetry collection. I think that mine is a unique style of writing that can appeal well beyond a *'pure poetry'* readership.

If you enjoyed it, I'd like to ask you to do two small things for me.

First, take a moment to find your favourite online retail store and leave a short review of the book in your preferred store.

Online reviews provide social proof to readers and are critical to Indie authors such as myself.

The second thing is, please pop over to my author page **www.FrankPrem.com**, and subscribe to receive my occasional Newsletter.

From time to time I'll let you know what is happening with myself and my writing, as well as keeping you informed of any giveaways I may be planning.

You can also find me on Facebook and Twitter
.

Other Published Works

Frank Prem

Small Town Kid (2018)

Devil In The Wind (2019)

The New Asylum (2019)

Herja, Devastation - With Cage Dunn (2019)

Walk Away Silver Heart (2020)

A Kiss for the Worthy (2020)

Rescue and Redemption (2020)

Pebbles to Poems (2020)

Picture Poetry/Spoken Image

Voices (In The Trash) (2020)

The Beechworth Bakery Bears (2021)

Sheep On The Somme (2021)

What Readers Say

Small Town Kid

A modern-day minstrel

Highly recommended

—A. F. (Australia)

Small-Town Kid is a wonderful collection

—S. T. (Australia)

A poet's walk through his childhood in a small Australian town.

—J. L. (USA)

Devil In The Wind

Instantly grips you by the throat in his step-by-step story of survival.

Bravo!

—K. K. (USA)

Very moving, beautiful, and terrible

—J. S. (South Africa)

Outstanding!

—B. T. (Australia)

The New Asylum

Brilliant succinct memoir.

__M.P-B. (Australia)

Words can't do justice to the emotional journey I travelled in (reading this collection).

__C. D. (Australia)

If I had to pick one book over the past year that has truly resonated with me, this would be it.

__K. B. (USA)

Walk Away Silver Heart

Has an extraordinary way with words and his poems invoke great passion and emotion in the reader.

—R C (United States)

As Memorable as My Favorite Music

—M D (United States)

Each response becomes a glimpse, and combined, they encapsulate a graceful reflection on a loving relationship.

A beautiful collection.

—D P (United States)

A Kiss For The Worthy

A Celebration of Life Written in Thoughtful Bursts of Poetic Expression

—C M C (United States)

A fascinating poetry collection!

Recommending to true poetry-lovers!

—A N I (United States)

With every verse, I found myself reflecting about myself, my life, and the world.

—K

Rescue and Redemption

The passion of love in its many forms explored by one for another.

—J L (United States)

Refresh your heart and mind

—S C (United States)

I've enjoyed every word, every breath. Every moment within the life of these stories.

—C D (Australia)

Herja, Devastation

Simply written, powerfully felt.

__C. (Australia)

This is a book I will reread and remember for a long, long time.

__C. (Australia)

As a combination of poetry, prose, and wonderfully ominous illustrations, I found Herja, Devastation refreshingly original.

Highly recommended!

—G. B. (Australia)

Index of Individual Poems

FrankPrem.com

www.ingramcontent.com/pod-product-compliance
Lightning Source LLC
Chambersburg PA
CBHW052019030426
42335CB00026B/3201